A PLACE APART

Houses of Christian Hospitality and Prayer in Europe

ENGLAND   IRELAND
SCOTLAND   WALES

Janet L. Joy

RAPHAEL PUBLISHING
P.O.Box 750
Milton, WA 98354

Liturgy of the Hours edited by the Poor Clare Monastery of Our Lady of Mercy, Belleville, IL, who also granted permission to use CLOCK OF PRAISE – copyright held by the monastery.

The publisher is grateful for permission to use the artwork of Poor Clare Nuns from Carlow, Ireland and Neath, Wales. Cover art by Poor Clare Nuns, Roswell, New Mexico, USA.

Library of Congress Catalog Card Number: 99-96114.

ISBN: 0-9673074-2-2

RAPHAEL PUBLISHING
P.O. Box 750
Milton, WA 98354

TABLE OF CONTENTS

To Gregory

INTRODUCTION

A PLACE APART – *England, Ireland, Scotland and Wales* – is a listing of select monasteries, convents, guest houses, retreat houses and places of pilgrimage for those who are seeking to enrich their time apart by spending a few hours, or days in a prayerful setting.

Individuals, families and groups taking a 'spiritual vacation' can expect a memorable experience, whether on retreat or simply choosing to stay in a Christian guest house while visiting Europe.

Most houses suggest that you contact them well in advance, giving specific dates to reserve, and any special needs. Upon inquiry, a booking form may be sent stating current tariffs or suggested donation as well as other pertinent information.

Current material sent to me was reviewed and summarized, and each house has authorized its publication under the present format, with some variations to meet the wishes of a particular house.

May God Bless your pilgrimage, and may it be one of Peace, Joy and Renewal.

Janet L. Joy

THE LITURGY OF THE HOURS

From ancient times, the Church has had the custom of celebrating each day the Liturgy of the Hours. In this way, the Church fulfills the Lord's precept to pray without ceasing, at once offering its praise to God the Father and interceding for the salvation of the world.
-Decree of Promulgation for the revised Liturgy of the Hours

In many monasteries, as the world sleeps, monks and nuns assemble in their chapels or churches to praise God. Their prayer, the Liturgy of the Hours (also known as the Divine Office or the *Opus Dei,* the Work of God), places them at the very heart of the praying Church.

For centuries, priests, monks and nuns have been entrusted with the official "prayer of the Hours," the Divine Office. The revision of the liturgy following the Second Vatican Council affirms this singular role of praise, while at the same time reminding the faithful that the Liturgy of the Hours is truly the prayer of the whole People of God, encouraging the laity to make use of the Liturgy of the Hours, either by praying some part of it in conjunction with a monastic community, or in their own parish, or even individually.

Traditionally there are seven canonical hours, rooting this ancient Christian prayer in the practices of the Chosen People, whose psalmist exultantly declared "Seven times a day I praise You!" (Ps. 119)

MATINS (also known as the Office of Readings, or Vigils) is the longest of the hours. There are still communities of monks and nuns that retain the ancient custom of praying this hour in the middle of the night, thus emphasizing its character as the first hour of the new day.

LAUDS is the Morning Prayer of the Church.

TERCE, SEXT and NONE are traditionally called "the little hours," and correspond to the customary Jewish times for prayer during the day – the third hour, the sixth hour, the

ninth hour, or, as the breviary now designates them:
Midmorning, Midday, Midafternoon.

     VESPERS is the Evening Prayer of the Church.

     COMPLINE, as the Latin name implies, is the Night
Prayer of the Church.

There are many ways of rendering the Liturgy of the Hours,
following the directives given by the Church and in keeping
with the particular customs of the various religious families.
Some communities will chant the Office on a single tone (recto-
tono), or use simple psalm tones, often composed by the monks
or nuns themselves. Others use a modal, non-metrical chant
composed specifically for the vernacular Office; still others use a
more elaborate, three-voice setting. The purpose of every Office
rendering remains the same: to offer to God a sacrifice of praise
and petition that is reverent, dignified and beautiful.

*The Liturgy of the Hours is the voice of the Bride addressing the
Bridegroom,* - Christ the Lord. (Sacrosanctum Concilium) The
Eucharistic Liturgy and the Liturgy of the Hours form the
spiritual framework around which the entire monastic life is
arranged. Monastic times of work, prayer, study, recreation as
well as the monastic practices of silence, asceticism, spiritual
reading and community life all flow out from and contribute to
this continual offering of holy praise.

The following CLOCK OF PRAISE, the daily horarium of the
Poor Clare Nuns, is offered as an example of how a typical
monastic day is built around the "Work of God" which is the
Liturgy.

"At midnight, I will rise to thank You!"
(Ps. 119)
In the life of Poor Clare nuns, Sister
Sacristan's bell sounds at 00:30, calling
them to choir for the Office of Matins,
and at 04:55 for Lauds – "With praise,
let us awake the dawn!" (Ps. 57)

A half hour of Eucharistic Adoration precedes Holy Mass at 07:00 – "What return can I make to the Lord for His goodness to me? I will offer a sacrifice of thanks and call upon His name!" (Ps. 116)

 The blessing of the Holy Spirit is invoked upon the whole Church during the Office of Terce at 08:00 – "Send forth your Spirit, and they shall be created!" (Ps. 104)

Then the works of the monastery morning begin – "Give success to the works of our hands." (Ps. 90)

At 10:45 the nuns file into choir for a period of spiritual reading leading into the Office of Sext. The Blessed Sacrament is reposed, and to the sound of a psalm, they go in procession to the refectory for their noon repast – "Give thanks to the Lord for He is good: for His love endures forever!" (Ps. 118)

After dinner and cleanup, individual study time lasts until the Office of None at 13:25 and Exposition of the Blessed Sacrament - "With all my voice, I cry to the Lord!" (Ps. 142)

At 16:10 the afternoon prayers and tasks are placed in God's hands as the bell summons the nuns to choir for Rosary, Vespers and Meditation – "Let my prayer rise before you like incense, the raising of my hands like the evening oblation." (Ps. 141)

A simple collation at 17:30 is followed by the Angelus and some free time for prayer and final chores and projects.

The bell calls the nuns to Recreation at 18:40, and the monastery echoes with the sounds of laughter and sisterly sharing – "How good and how pleasant it is when brothers live in unity!" (Ps. 131)

Stillness settles in at 19:40 when the bell announces night prayers and the Office of Compline, ending with the singing of the final antiphon to Our Lady.

By 20:45, the Poor Clares retire and The Great Silence envelops the monastery, broken only by the bell resounding through the halls as another Poor Clare day begins – "At midnight, a cry is heard: Behold, the Bridegroom comes; go out to meet Him!"
(Matt. 25:6)

"Behold Him
Consider Him
Contemplate Him
Desire to imitate Him"

Letter of St. Clare.

England

Alton Abbey   Tel: 01420 562 145/563 575
King's Hill, Beech   Fax: 01420 561691
Alton
Hampshire GU34 4AP
Benedictine Community of Our Lady and St. John

Open To: Individuals, groups for Retreats, or simply for a peaceful time apart. Weekend Retreats conducted by the monks. Spiritual Direction available.

Accommodation: Hospitality is provided in the Guest House in 16 single bedrooms. Meals taken with the monks. Breakfast self-service. Also, self-catering flat available.

Guests Admitted To: Abbey Church (1905) to join the monks for liturgical services. Grounds.

Of Interest: This small Benedictine Community of men, founded in 1895, began by working with merchant seamen in foreign ports. Today they provide hospitality, pastoral care, and support at the Abbey for those in need of their assistance.

Access: Road: M3 from Odiham, then B3348 to A339 and follow signs to the Abbey. A32 from Fareham through Alton. A31 from Winchester through Alton.

Rydal Hall, Carlisle Diocesan Retreat and Conference Center
Ambleside   Tel: 015394 32050
Cumbria LA22 9LX   Fax: 015394 34887
E-mail:rydalhall@aol.com Contact: Retreat Secretary

Open To: Individuals, groups, families for Retreats, Educational and Professional Training, School and College visits, and Holidays.

Accommodation: Hospitality is provided for 56 persons in single, twin-bedded, and family rooms. Drawing room, library, meeting rooms, conference room, licensed bar, summer house. A converted barn in the grounds is suitable for large gatherings. Self-catering youth center (36 beds). Also, campsite available.

Guests Admitted To: Chapel. Gift/Book Shop. St. Mary Rydal Church.

Of Interest: Rydal Hall is home to a small Christian Ecumenical Community who pledge themselves to follow Our Lord's example of loving and willing service. This elegant 17th c. Georgian mansion is set in thirty acres of beautiful grounds with woodland and a waterfall – an excellent base from which to walk and climb. Located in the heart of the English Lakes District, it is sheltered on three sides by the fells, with superb views down to Windermere.

Access: Good public transport.

Aylesford Priory – The Friars
Aylesford, Maidstone
Kent ME20 7BX
Roman Catholic Carmelite

Tel: 01622 717272
Fax: 01622 715575
Contact: Guest Sister

Open To: Individuals, groups, families for Retreats, Courses, both residential and non-residential. Guests may request a meeting with one of the Friars. Guided Tours weekdays.

Accommodation: Hospitality is provided in the Guest House, B&B or full board. Set meal times. Max. length of stay 2 wks.

Guests Admitted To: Monastery Church to join the Community for liturgical services. Library. Tea Room and Book Shop. Grounds.

Of Interest: This Pilgrimage Center, situated in the country by the River Medway, is a blend of medieval and modern. The chapels contain outstanding modern works of religious art. Pilgrims are welcome on Sundays and during the week, and may watch as pottery is made – sold on the premises.

Access: Rail: To Aylesford Sta. Road: A20 from London or Maidstone. Maidstone 4.8 km.

The Ammerdown Center   Tel: 01761 433709
Radstock   Fax: 01761 433094
Bath BA3 5SW
E-mail:centre@ammerdown.freeserve.co.wk

Open To: Individuals, groups for Retreats or simply a quiet time away. Residential and day use. Spiritual Direction available. All are welcome.

Accommodation: Hospitality is provided in the Center. Adjacent to the Main Center are self-catering single and double flatlets.

Guests Admitted To: Chapel. Grounds.

Of Interest: The Ammerdown Center is situated within easy distance of Wells, Glastonbury, Bath, Bristol and the West Country.

Access: Good public transport.

Priory of Our Lady of Peace
Turvey
Bedford MK43 8DE
Roman Catholic Benedictine

Tel: 01234 881432
Fax: 01234 881538
Contact: Retreat Secretary

Open To: Individuals for Retreats or simply a quiet time apart.

Accommodation: Hospitality is provided in the Priory in 5 single, 4 twin-bedded rooms.

Guests Admitted To: Chapel. Christians and those of other faiths who truly seek God are welcome to join the Sisters in prayer. Library. Gardens.

Of Interest: Prayer forms the basis of the Sisters' lives, and affects every aspect of their work and relationship with society. By developing a deep spiritual awareness of the unity of all creation, and of the simple beauty of everyday life, they seek in their work and prayer, especially their liturgy, to radiate God's life and peace to all who visit their monastery.

Access: Road: A428. Buses X2 and X3 Bedford-Northampton. Stop is near the monastery. Bedford 12.8 km.

Canterbury Cathedral
Cathedral House
11 The Precincts
Canterbury
Kent CT1 2EH
Anglican

Tel: 01227 762862
Fax: 01227 865222
Contact: Director of Visits

Open To: Pilgrims/tourists year round. Group pilgrimages and special guided tours booked in advance.

Accommodation: Day facilities in the Education Center for school groups and other organizations. Contact the Education Officer for full info. Cafes/restaurants closeby.

Visitors Admitted To: The Crypt – Chapel of Our Lady Undercroft. Chapel of Our Lady Martyrdom (NW transept near site of the martyrdom of St. Thomas Becket (1170). Audio-visual presentation in Theodore (NW corner of the Great Cloister) – Feb.-Oct. Cathedral Shops. Archives and Library open for research by appointment. Concerts/dramas/exhibitions.

Of Interest: Canterbury Cathedral has been a center of pilgrimage for centuries, even before the death of Thomas Becket. The Mission of the Cathedral is to encourage a living faith by interpreting the Gospel through the Cathedral building itself, its history, its saints, its worship, preaching and teaching, and through community service.

Access: Rail: Canterbury E Sta. Or W Sta., then by bus. Good public transport. Park and ride.

The Monastery of the Holy Trinity   Tel: 01342 712074
Crawley Down, **Crawley**   Contact: Guest Brother
West Sussex RH10 4LH
Anglican
The Community of the Servants of the Will of God

Open To: Individuals for Retreats or a time of rest and renewal.

Accommodation: Hospitality is provided in the Monastery in 11 bedrooms. Meals taken with the Community.

Guests Admitted To: Chapel to join the monks for worship services. Grounds.

Of Interest: The Monastery of the Holy Trinity, situated in good walking country, offers peaceful surroundings that are conducive to a prayerful time apart.

Access: Good public transport.

Holland House Retreat, Conference, and Laity Center
Cropthorne, Pershore   Tel: 081 386 860330
Worcestershire WR10 3NB   Fax: 081 386 861208
E-mail:laycentre@surfaid.org   Contact: The Warden

Open To: Individuals, groups for Retreats, Conferences, Holidays. Guests are welcome on space-available basis during group offerings. Short-notice stay possible.

Accommodation: Hospitality is provided in 18 single bedrooms, 6 twin-bedded, all with sinks. Meals provided for groups (available for individuals).

Guests Admitted To: Chapel. Library. Grounds.

Of Interest: This 17th c. house, situated along the River Avon, is linked to other centers in Europe through the European Association of Academies and Laity Centers. They work mostly with the laity to discover deeper insights into their Christian calling within churches and the world.

Access: Rail: Evesham or Pershore Sta., then by car or bus. Road: M5, exit onto 4104 to Pershore, then A44 to Cropthorne. M40 from Stow and Oxford.

As for me,
I trust in Your
merciful love ...
Psalm 12.

The Sozein Trust
The Old Vicarage
Church Lane
Horsley Woodhouse
Derby DE7 6BB

Tel: 01332 780598
Contact: The Director

Open To: Individuals, groups for Contemplative Retreats and a few quiet days for rest and renewal. Spiritual Direction available. Day use for up to 15 persons.

Accommodation: Hospitality is provided for up to 3 persons in 2 bedrooms. Shared meals and fellowship. Library. Prayer room.

Guests Admitted To: Grounds.

Of Interest: The Sozein Trust, a unique Derbyshire Ministry of Healing Project, welcomes persons seeking ministry through prayer and quiet. The Old Vicarage is located in an area of great beauty near the Peak District National Park, with easy access to Nottingham (Sherwood Forest) and Birmingham.

Access: Rail: British Rail services – London 2 hrs., Birmingham 1 hr. Road: A608 from Derby, turn off at A609 (Horsley Woodhouse) in direction of Kilburn and Belper.

The House of Prayer
35 Seymour Road
East Molesey
Surrey KT8 0PB
Roman Catholic Srs. of the Christian Retreat

Tel: 0181 941 2313
Contact: Retreat Secretary

Open To: Individuals for Retreats. Groups for Days of Prayer. Spiritual Direction and Counseling available. All are welcome.

Accommodation: Hospitality is provided in 4 self-catering hermitages. The House of Prayer has several large group rooms, prayer room, library.

Guests Admitted To: Chapel. Grounds.

Of Interest: The experienced staff of the House of Prayer has teams that are prepared to provide programs at other locations.

Access: Air: Heathrow Airport 19.2 km. Rail: Nearest Sta. Hampton Court.

My heart and my soul ring out their joy to God the living God!
Psalm 83.

Community of St. Mary at the Cross   Tel: 0181 958 7868
Priory Field Drive   Fax: 0181 958 1920
Edgware   Contact: Guest Sister
Middlesex HA8 9PZ
Anglican Benedictine

Open To: Individuals, groups for 'Monastic Experience', Retreats, Meetings, Conferences, Family Celebrations, Holidays. Sisters available for conversation and listening. Reference needed from someone in ministry at time of booking if not known to the Sisters.

Accommodation: Hospitality is provided in the two-story Guest House 'Loreto' in 7 bedrooms. Max. stay 2 wks. Also, the Hermitage, a small flatlet. Meals taken in Convent refectory or in Henry Nihill House.

Guests Admitted To: Convent Church. Grounds.

Of Interest: This Benedictine Order of Nuns has been engaged in the caring ministry since 1866. The Care Center opened in 1992, and the Conference Center in 1994. Henry Nihill House, located in the Convent grounds, provides high-quality care of the disabled and elderly. The residents enjoy the benefits of the special monastic ethos and join in the worship of the Community.

Access: Air: Heathrow Airport 32 km. Rail: British Mill Hill, St. Pancras Line. London Underground City of London Branch on Northern Line to Edgware Sta. Road: 1.6 km. From M1, Jct. 4, and A1. London 19.2 km.

National Shrine of St. Jude
Whitefriars
Tanners Street, **Faversham**
Kent ME13 7JN
Roman Catholic Carmelite

Tel/Fax: 0795 539214
Contact: Shrine Director

Open To: Individuals, families, groups for Mass and Devotions. Special services arranged for groups with prior notice.

Accommodation: Non-residential services.

Visitors Admitted To: Parish Church of Our Lady of Mount Carmel. St. Jude Shrine. Small Meditation Garden.

Of Interest: The complex includes the Carmelite Priory (1740), the Church (1869) – formerly a Quaker school, the Carmelite newsletter office, and a printing works used by a commercial firm.

Access: Rail: BR Sta. Closeby. Road: M2, exit 6 to A251. Take L onto A2, R onto Ospringe Rd. which becomes South Rd. Then take L onto Napleton Rd. and L on Tanners St. (one way).

Prinknash Abbey
Cranham
Gloucester GL4 8EX
Tel: 01452 812455
Fax: 01452 813305
Contact: Guestmaster
Roman Catholic Benedictine

St. Peter's Grange
Prinknash Abbey
Tel: 01452 813592
Fax: 01452 814189
Contact: The Warden

Open To: Men to the Abbey Guest House. Men and women to The Grange. Private and group Retreats, Day Events. Groups bring their own leader, but may contact Fr. Abbot if they wish a monk to lead a retreat.

Accommodation: Hospitality is provided in the Abbey Guest House in 8 single rooms. Meals taken with the monks in the refectory. The Grange can accommodate up to 35 if all rooms are shared, or 13 single. Meeting rooms, dining room. Quiet prevails, especially after 21:30.

Guests Admitted To: Abbey Church to join the monks for Mass and the Divine Office. Grange Chapel. Grounds.

Of Interest: The Abbey sponsors two special retreats; one for Advent and one for Pentecost, conducted by a member of the Community and a Dominican Nun, in St. Peter's Grange which is three quarters of a mile across the estate from the Abbey.

Access: Rail: Bus and coach stations at Gloucester (8 km.) and Cheltenham (12.8 km.). Infrequent local buses. Road: From M5, Jct. 11A, A117 to A16 turn S (right). From M4, Jct. 15, A419/417 to A46 turn S (left).

Grace and Compassion Benedictines
Retreat and Holiday Houses

St. Benedict's
1 Manor Road
Kemp Town, **Brighton**
East Sussex BN2 5EA
Roman Catholic

Tel: 01273 674140
Contact: Superior

Open To: Individuals, families, small groups.

Accommodation: Hospitality is provided in 3 flats (13 bedrooms), some en-suite, for 18 persons. Dining room, sitting rooms, conference room, library. Self-catering, B&B or full board.

Guests Admitted To: Chapel. Daily Mass available. Garden.

Of Interest: St. Benedict's is located near the sea.

Access: Road: On bus route.

St. Mary's Dower, St. Mary's House
38 Preston Park Avenue
Brighton
East Sussex BN1 6HG

Tel: 01273 556035
Contact: Superior

Open To: Individuals, married couples, families.

Accommodation: Hospitality is provided in 4 bedrooms, some en-suite, for 6 persons. Self-catering, B&B, or full board.

Guests Admitted To: House Chapel. Daily Mass available.

Of Interest: St. Mary's is located in a quiet location in the grounds of a Home for the Elderly near a bus route.

Holy Cross Priory
Cross-in-Hand
Heathfield
East Sussex TN21 0TS

Tel: 01435 863298
Contact: Prioress

Open To: Persons seeking accommodation in a convent setting.

Accommodation: Hospitality is provided in the guest facilities, full board.

Guests Admitted To: Chapel for daily Mass. Grounds.

Of Interest: This is the Novitiate House of the Grace and Compassion Benedictines. A Home for the Elderly is also in the grounds. Contact for further information.

Holiday House
27/79 Holloway
Malmesbury
Wiltshire

Contact: Superior
More Hall Convent
Randwick, Stroud
Gloucester GL6 6EP

Open To: Individuals, married couples, families.

Accommodation: Hospitality is provided in 2 self-catering cottages (4 bedrooms total) for 6 persons.

Guests Admitted To: Local churches.

Of Interest: The Holiday House is located in a quiet, picturesque area close to churches near the town center. Contact for further information.

Convents With Some Guest Accommodation

St. Joseph's   Tel: 01243 864051
Albert Road   Contact: Superior
Bognor Regis
West Sussex PO21 1NJ

Montana   Tel: 01284 787321
Great Barton   Contact: Superior
Near **Bury St. Edmunds**
Suffolk IP31 2RF

Grace and Compassion Convent
Paddockhurst Road   Tel: 01342 715672
Turners Hill, **Crawley**   Contact: Superior
West Sussex RH10 4GZ

More Hall Convent   Tel: 01453 764486
Randwick, **Stroud**   Contact: Superior
Gloucestershire GL6 6EP

All Convents open year round. Full Board.
Daily Mass available.

Grace and Compassion Houses for the Elderly
Run by Lay People
With Some Guest Accommodation

Dawes House
Burwash
East Sussex TN19 7HD

Tel: 01435 882026
Contact: Housekeeper for
details

Our Lady's Flats
Eythorne, **Dover**
Kent CT15 4AE

Contact: Housekeeper

Garson House
Lee Road
Lynton
North Devon EX35 6HU

Tel: 01598 753202
Contact: Matron for details

From the rising of the sun to its setting Praised be the name of the Lord!

Chapel House
Burrswood
Groombridge
Tunbridge Wells
Kent TN3 9PY
Church of England

Tel: 01892 863818
Fax: 01892 862597
Contact: The Admissions
Secretary

Open To: Individuals, groups, families for Retreats, Conferences, Holidays. Informal Spiritual Direction available. Full-time hostess to enable guests to make the most of their stay.

Accommodation: Hospitality is provided in Chapel House for 16 persons in single and double bedrooms, all en-suite. Breakfast brought to the rooms; other meals in main house. Self-catering kitchen available for light meals. Packed lunches on request. A conference room in Burrswood can accommodate 45 persons for day use.

Guests Admitted To: Church of Christ the Healer. Four healing services each week. Public welcome. House chapel.

Of Interest: Burrswood was established as a Christian Healing Center in 1948, and has a small inpatient wing and an outpatient wing. Chapel House, adjacent to but quite separate from the Center, was originally the private family home for Burrswood's founder. It is set in two hundred and twenty acres of peaceful grounds, including a croquet lawn, all-weather tennis court, woodlands, meadows, pond and flower gardens. The Sussex Border Path and the Wealdway Path cross the estate, making Burrswood an ideal stop-over or base for a walking holiday. Guests may use the hydrotherapy pool and physiotherapy suite for a small fee.

Access: Air: Gatwick and Heathrow Airports. Rail: London Charing Cross to Tunbridge Wells, then by bus to Groombridge (M-Fri.). Road: Close to M25. Pick-up at RR Sta. or airport can be arranged at competitive rates.

Trelowarren Christian Fellowship   Tel: 01326 221366
Mawgan-in-Meneage, **Helston**   Contact: The Warden
Cornwall TR12 6AD

Open To: Individuals for Retreats or a quiet, restful Holiday. Spiritual Direction available.

Accommodation: Hospitality is provided for 23 persons in single, double and family bedrooms, some with wash basins. Shared bathrooms. Breakfast and evening meal included.

Guests Admitted To: Chapel to join the Community for morning and evening prayer. Grounds.

Of Interest: Trelowarren Christian Fellowship is a small Christian Community, residing in this ancient manor house. The Market Town of Helston is on the Lizard Peninsula, a popular resort area. Lizard Head is the southernmost point of Great Britain. The lovely South Cornwall scenery includes several lighthouses. An extended woodland walk from the house leads to the Helford River.

Access: Road: Helston 8 km. Falmouth 17.6 km. Pick-up from Helston possible with advance notice.

St. Francis House
Hemingford Grey
Huntingdon
Cambs PE18 9BJ
The Community of the Resurrection

Tel: 01480 462185
Contact: The Warden

Open To: Individuals, groups seeking spiritual refreshment in a peaceful environment. Open Guided Retreats arranged during the year.

Accommodation: Hospitality is provided in 17 single bedrooms, 3 twin-bedded. Dining room, lounge, library, reading room.

Guests Admitted To: Chapel. Garden.

Of Interest: From the picturesque village of Hemingford Grey, there are pleasant walks along the river and in local meadows.

Access: Rail: Huntingdon Sta., then taxi or local bus. Road: A14.

St. Cecilia's Abbey   Tel/Fax: 01983 562602
Appley Rise, Ryde   Contact: Guest Mistress
Isle of Wight PO33 1LH
Roman Catholic Benedictine

Open To: Women, married couples, small groups for
Non-Directed Retreats, with the opportunity to speak with one
of the Sisters. Young women discerning a call to religious life
may spend time in the enclosure with the Community.

Accommodation: Hospitality is provided in The Garth in 3
twin-bedded rooms, shower, self-catering, fully-equipped
kitchen, sitting room, small library. Also, the main Retreat
House has an annex available to guests. Max. stay 1 wk.

Guests Admitted To: Monastery Church to join the Nuns for
Mass and Divine Office, sung in Latin Gregorian Chant.

Of Interest: Restoration of monastic life began in France in
1833 in an abandoned 12th c. Priory of Solesmes. Today the
Abbey of St. Pierre is the Motherhouse of the Solesmes
Congregation of monks and nuns. St. Cecilia's became part of
this International Congregation in 1950, and is under the
patronage of the Peace of the Sacred Heart. The Abbey and
Guest House are situated close to the sea.

Access: Ferry: Portsmouth Harbor – Fishbourne, then a 20
min. drive. BR/Coach – Portsmouth Harbor. Hovercraft or
catamaran to Ryde Esplanade, then a 20 min. walk or taxi.

Bridgettine Guest House   Tel: 0753 662645 or 662073
Fulmer Common Road   Contact: Guest Sister
Iver Heath
Buckfastleigh SL0 0NR
Roman Catholic Order of Our Most Holy Savior

Open To: Individuals, groups for Retreats, Conferences, Ecumenical Meetings, Days of Recollection, and Spiritual Holidays.

Accommodation: Hospitality is provided in the Guest House in single and double bedrooms with baths or showers and WC. Dining room, conference center, library.

Guests Admitted To: Chapel. Grounds.

Of Interest: In 1931, five Sisters were sent here by their Abbess in Rome, Mother Elisabeth Hesselblad, to open a House of Hospitality and Prayer for all. The small house was eventually enlarged, and it is situated on a quiet road not far from Uxbridge. Woodlands and a country lane, leading to the historic village of Fulmer, are behind the Guest House.

Access: Air: London Airport, then Green Line 727 to Uxbridge, 457 to Stag and Hounds, then walk to the Convent. Rail: Paddington-Slough Sta. Subway: London to Uxbridge.

Cenacle Retreat and Conference Center
Lance Lane   Tel: 0151 7222271/2
Liverpool L15 6TW   Contact: Retreat Secretary
Roman Catholic Srs. of Our Lady of the Cenacle

Open To: Individuals, groups for Retreats, Conferences, residential and non-residential use. Spiritual Direction available.

Accommodation: Hospitality is provided in the Retreat House in 2 bedrooms. Meals taken in dining room with non-residential groups.

Guests Admitted To: Chapel. Grounds.

Of Interest: The main apostolate of the Srs. of O.L. of the Cenacle is retreat work. A visit to the Liverpool Cathedral, the largest in England, is strongly recommended.

Access: Road: M62. Buses from City Center.

Benedictine Center for Spirituality   Tel: 0181 449 2499
29 Bramley Road   Fax: 0181 449 2499
London N14 4HE   Contact: The Secretary
Roman Catholic Monks of the Olivetan Congregation

Open To: Individuals, groups for Retreats, Courses, and Quiet Days. Spiritual Direction available. Center facilities also available to those who share the same aims as the Community.

Accommodation: Hospitality is provided in 2 single, 3 double bedrooms. Larger groups accommodated in the Monastery Guest House. Midday meal taken with the monks in the refectory. Conference rooms.

Guests Admitted To: Benedictine Parish Church of Christ the King.

Of Interest: The Center is situated on the edge of the countryside. A six hundred acre park is nearby for quiet walks.

Access: Rail: Piccadilly Line to Oakwood Underground Sta., then a five-min. walk. Road: M25, Jct. 24, S on A111 for 4.8 km. To A110 (Enfield). Located between A110 and Oakwood Sta. #307 bus stops outside the church.

Marie Reparatrice Retreat Center   Tel: 0181 946 1088
115 Ridgway   Fax: 0181 947 9820
Wimbledon   Contact: Retreat
London SW19 4RB   Secretary
Roman Catholic Srs. of Marie Reparatrice

Open To: Individuals, groups for Retreats, Days of
Recollection, Prayer Evenings, and for those wishing a restful
time apart. Spiritual Direction available.

Accommodation: Hospitality is provided in the Retreat
Center in single bedrooms with wash basins. Shared
bathrooms. Prayer room, library. Guests are asked to maintain
a prayerful attitude in the house.

Guests Admitted To: Chapel to join the Sisters for daily Mass
and Divine Office. Adoration of the Blessed Sacrament. Parish
Church nearby.

Of Interest: The Congregation of the Srs. of Marie Reparatrice
was founded in 1855. Their main apostolate is retreat work,
and their spirituality is Ignatian.

Access: Road: Jct. of Ridgway and Edge Hill.

More House
53 Cromwell Road
South Kensington
London SW7 2EH
Roman Catholic

Tel: 0171 584 2040
Fax: 0171 581 5748
E-mail:0171 589 4228
Contact: The Warden

Open To: Visitors to London during July and August.
Meetings/Conferences in Thomas More Room.

Accommodation: Hospitality is provided in 38 single
bedrooms, 20 double, some triple, and dormitories.
Bathrooms/showers each floor. B&B. Meals served in dining
room.

Guests Admitted To: Chapel for daily Mass. When Chaplains
on holiday, visiting priests say Mass.

Of Interest: This large Victorian building is the Hall of
Residence for students attending London University Colleges,
and is the West College Catholic Chaplaincy Center. It is
situated close to the National History and Victoria and Albert
Museums, and is a five-minute walk to Kensington Gardens and
Hyde Park.

Access: Road: A1 at the crossroads of Cromwell Rd. and
Queen's Gate.

Newman House
111 Gower St.
London WC1E 6AR
Roman Catholic

Tel: 0171 387 6370
Fax: 0171 388 6430
Contact: Administrator

Open To: Visitors seeking a quiet place to stay in April and June to Sept. House ethos must be respected.

Accommodation: Hospitality is provided in 63 single student bedrooms (some twin-bedded). Showers/bathrooms each floor. Simple breakfast served in dining room. Self-catering available in kitchens. Meeting rooms, 2 small conference rooms, library.

Guests Admitted To: Chapel for Mass. Visiting priests may celebrate Mass by arrangement.

Of Interest: Newman House is the Chaplaincy Center for students at London's universities and home to 63 students during the academic year. It is within walking distance of many of the sights in London.

Access: Rail: Euston Sta. Underground: Euston Sq., Warren St., Goodge St. Road: Located between University St. and Torrington Pl. Buses 10, 24, 27 and 73.

Tyburn Convent   Tel: 0171 723 7262
Shrine of the Sacred Heart and the Tyburn Martyrs
8 Hyde Park Place   Contact: Guest Sister
London W2 2LJ
Roman Catholic Benedictine
Adorers of the Sacred Heart of Jesus of Montmartre

Open To: Women for Retreat, or simply share in the quiet and prayerful life of the Community. Booking by letter.

Accommodation: Hospitality is provided in the Guest House in 6 single bedrooms. Meals taken in dining room.

Guests Admitted To: Chapel to join the Sisters for liturgical services. Perpetual Adoration of the Blessed Sacrament and Night Adoration. Guided tours of the Shrine three times a day.

Of Interest: The Crypt of the Martyrs Pilgrimage Center perpetuates the memory of one hundred and five Catholic Martyrs of the Reformation period who died on this spot.

Access: Rail: Bayswater Rd. Sta. close to Convent. Road: Located near intersection of Hyde Park Pl. and Stanhope Pl.

All Hallows
Rouen Road
Norwich NR1 1QT
Anglican Community of the Sacred Passion

Tel: 01603 624738
Contact: Guest Sister

Open To: Individuals for Retreats or a quiet break.

Accommodation: Hospitality is provided in the Convent for 6 persons in single or twin-bedded rooms. Upon application, indicate B&B only or if evening meal is also desired.

Guests Admitted To: House Chapel. St. Julian's Church.

Of Interest: All Hallows adjoins St. Julian's Church and Shrine, associated with Mother Julian of Norwich. It is situated beside a busy road near the City Center and the Cathedral.

Access: Good public transport.

Carmelite Monastery
Quidenham
Norwich NR16 2PH
Roman Catholic

Tel: 01953 887202
Contact: Guest Sister

Open To: Individuals for Retreats. Guests structure their own time.

Accommodation: Hospitality is provided in 3 self-catering flats for 1 to 2 persons. Basic foods stocked.

Guests Admitted To: Small Chapel facing the Nuns' choir for Mass and Divine Office.

Of Interest: This Carmelite Monastery was founded in 1948. For many years Quidenham Hall was the home of the Earls of Albemarle. The original building dates back to 1609, but over the years, additions and alterations have been made. It is situated in the heart of lovely rural Norfolk, and the Sisters have fields that are open to visitors for quiet country walks.

Access: Rail: Nearest stations in Diss, Thetford, Attleborough. Road: A11, approx. 32 km. SW of Norwich.

Burford Priory   Tel: 01993 823141
Priory Lane, Burford
Oxford OX18 4SQ
Anglican Benedictine
The Society of the Salutation of Mary the Virgin

Open To: Individuals, groups wishing to spend a time of
silence and reflection in a spiritual environment. Spiritual
Direction or conversing with a member of the Community
available by prior arrangement.

Accommodation: Hospitality is provided in the 16th c. Guest
House in 8 rooms (12 persons), wash basins. Shared
bathrooms/showers. Kitchen, dining room – self-serve
breakfast. Dinner and supper taken with the Community in the
refectory. Small conference room, oratory.

Guests Admitted To: Chapel to join the Community for
worship services. Lenthall Chapel (1662). Grounds.

Of Interest: Burford Priory is a mixed Community of nuns and
monks that seeks to support itself in a variety of ways such as
printing, icon-mounting, writing, and hospitality. It is situated
along the River Windrush on the edge of the Cotswolds.

Access: Rail: Charlbury Sta., Oxford to Hereford Line, then by
taxi. Some through trains from Paddington. Burford 12.8 km.
from station. Road: North of A40 Oxford to Cheltenham Rd.
Public transport limited to Burford or Carterton (6.4 km.).

St. Mary's Priory Tel: 01367 240133
Fernham, Faringdon Contact: Guest Mistress
Oxford SN7 7PP by letter
Roman Catholic Benedictine

Open To: Individuals, small groups for Retreats.

Accommodation: Hospitality is provided in St. Gabriel's
Retreat House in 2 twin-bedded rooms and 2 with 2 bunks,
wash basin in each room. Larger numbers occasionally
accommodated using their own sleeping bags. Shower,
kitchen/dining area, utility room, sitting room.

Guests Admitted To: Monastery Church to join the Sisters for
liturgical services. Grounds that are open to guests.

Of Interest: The Scandinavian style log Retreat House was
built in 1991 in the grounds of this rural monastery. It is
surrounded by farmland, and there are sites of historical and
archaeological interest accessible by car.

Access: Road: Buses from Swindon, 17.6km. and Oxford,
28.8 km. M-Sat., but infrequent service. Also, bus to Faringdon,
then by taxi 4.8 km.

The Cherwell Center
14/16 Norham Gardens
Oxford OX2 6QB
E-mail:cherwell@enterprise.net
Roman Catholic Society of the Holy Child Jesus

Tel: 01865 552106
Fax: 01865 558183
Contact: Director

Open To: Groups for residential and non-residential programs. Also, Individually-Guided Retreats with prior arrangement. Spiritual Direction.

Accommodation: Hospitality is provided in the Center in 13 single bedrooms, 8 double. Conference and meeting rooms.

Guests Admitted To: Chapel. Grounds.

Of Interest: The Society of the Holy Child Jesus is an International Community of Catholic women religious, founded in England in 1846 by an American, Cornelia Connelly. She and her companions responded to the wants of the age by developing a new vision of education for girls and young women, in a spirit of freedom and trust. At the Center, the team and others work to provide a place of Christ-centered hospitality in an atmosphere of freedom and peace. It is adjacent to University Parks, and Oxford City Center is a ten-minute walk away.

Access: Road: M40, A40 from London. M40 from Birmingham. A40 from Cheltenham. Located off Parks Rd. or Banbury Rd. Good public transport and park and ride. No parking at Cherwell, and restricted parking on surrounding streets.

Loyola Hall Jesuit and Spirituality Center
Warrington Road, Rainhill   Tel: 0151 426 4137
Prescot, Merseyside L35 6NZ   Fax: 0151 431 0115
E-mail:loyola@clara.net   Contact: Director
http:home.clara.net/loyola
Roman Catholic

Open To: Individuals, groups for 30-Day Retreats on the
Spiritual Exercises of St. Ignatius. Individually-Guided
Retreats, or a Short-Guided Retreat. Also, Courses in Ignatian
Spirituality. Day and residential use of facilities for Retreats,
Conferences, Meetings for groups who bring their own program.
Contact for further information and current program.

Accommodation: Hospitality is provided in Loyola Hall in 45
single bedrooms with wash basins, full board. Also, 15 beds in 4
and 5-bed attic rms. Dining rm., conference rms., lounges,
meeting rms., prayer rms., art rm., sauna, jacuzzi, massage rm.,
exercise equipment. *Accommodation changes in 2001 to: 41
single rms. With en-suite facilities. 2 twin and two 4-bed rms.*

Guests Admitted To: House Chapel. Gift Shop. Grounds.

Of Interest: Loyola Hall was established by the Jesuit Order
in 1923 and is ecumenical in its outreach to those who are
seeking to deepen their relationship with God. It is situated in
large beautiful grounds, ideal for quiet walks. The Port of
Liverpool, historic Chester, Manchester, the Welsh countryside,
and the English Lakes district are nearby for those wishing to
take an excursion during breaks. There is time between courses
to take the ferry or fly to Dublin, or visit London. Staff is
available to help with travel plans.

Access: Air: Manchester International Airport a 35 min. drive.
Liverpool Airport 20 min. Rail: Rainhill Sta. (a 20 min. walk).
Direct trains to Liverpool, Manchester, Chester, Warrington
Bank Quay for the West Coast Mainline and Wakefield. Local
bus service. Road: M62, Jct. 7. Bradford Leeds or Preston
approx. 1 hr. London and Glasgow about 4 hrs. A57, 20 min.
from Liverpool, 35 min. from Manchester.

Shepherds Dene Retreat House and Conference Center
Riding Mill   Tel: 01434 682212
Northumberland NE44 6AF   Fax: 01434 682311
                                         Contact: The Warden
E-mail:shepherdsdene@newcastle.anglican.org

Open To: Groups for Retreats, Conferences and Holidays. Residential and day use. Individuals at certain times.

Accommodation: Hospitality is provided in the main House in 13 twin rooms, 8 single. Also, 2 bedrooms in separate cottage available to rent on a self-catering basis.

Guests Admitted To: Grounds.

Of Interest: Shepherds Dene is located in rural Tynedale thirty-two kilometers from Newcastle upon Tyne. It is ideally situated for excursions to ancient Roman sites, the Scottish border and Lindisfarne, the cradle of Northumbria's Christianity.

Access: Easy access by road or public transport.

Wydale York Diocesan Center   Tel: 01723 859270
Brompton by Sawdon   Fax: 01723 859702
Scarborough   Contact: The Warden
North Yorkshire YO13 9DG

Open To: Individuals, groups for Retreats, Conferences and
Holidays.

Accommodation: Hospitality is provided in 34 bedrooms – 66
beds if shared. Bathrooms/showers each floor. Conference
room, dining room, lounge, sitting room, library, games room.
Self-catering dormitory accommodations available in Emmaus
Center, plus 4 ground floor bedrooms with wheelchair access for
16 guests.

Guests Admitted To: Chapel. Grounds.

Of Interest: Wydale Hall is situated in an area known for its
interesting walks. Details and certificates are available from
the staff. Wydale Walk is a thirty-two kilometer walk between
Wydale and Robin Hood's Bay.

Access: Rail: Snainton Sta. or Brompton Sta., then by bus.

Brook Place Ecumenical Center Tel/Fax: 01276 857561
Bagshot Road Contact: The Warden
Chobham
Surrey GU24 8SJ

Open To: Individuals, groups for Day Retreats, Meetings, Away-Days. Available to groups (min. 8 persons) for Residential Retreats, Workshops, Meetings.

Accommodation: Hospitality is provided in Brook Place House in 7 twin and 1 double bedroom (max. 16 guests). Dining room, lounge, library. Also, for larger day groups, the Tithe Barn can accommodate 70. Catering available for both places.

Guests Admitted To: Granary Chapel. Grounds.

Of Interest: Brook Place House and the Tithe Barn are 17th c. buildings with many original features, set in twenty-three acres of beautiful gardens and grounds.

Access: Rail: Woking Sta., then by taxi. Frequent train services from London Waterloo.

The Shrine of Our Lady of Walsingham
The College, **Walsingham**
Norfolk NR22 6EE   Tel/Fax: 01328 820266
Anglican   Contact: The Administrator

Open To: Pilgrims visiting this ancient Shrine. Special
Weekend Services Easter through October. Schedule sent on
request.

Accommodation: Hospitality is provided for pilgrims
Feb. – Dec. Contact: The Bursar, The Shrine Office,
Walsingham, Norfolk NR22 6EE. Meals at set times daily.

Guests Admitted To: During Pilgrimage Season: Daily Mass,
Sprinkling at the Well, Evening and Shrine Prayers. Grounds.

Of Interest: The heart of Walsingham is the Holy House,
England's Nazareth. Inspired by Mary's pilgrimage of faith,
pilgrims come to this place of peace, silence and adoration
seeking conversion and renewal.

Access: Rail: King's Cross to King's Lynn, then bus or taxi.

Order of the Holy Paraclete
St. Hilda's Priory
Sneaton Castle, **Whitby**
North Yorks YO21 3QN
E-mail:ohppriorywhitby@btinternet.com
Anglican

Tel: 01947 602079
Fax: 01947 820854
Contact: Guest Sister

Open To: Individuals for Retreats or a quiet time apart.
Opportunity to speak with one of the Sisters as desired.

Accommodation: Hospitality is provided on the Visitors
Landing in the Priory in 2 bedrooms. Meals taken with the
Community. Also, accommodation in the Lodge (4 bedrooms)
and The Terrace (3 bedrooms). Self-catering or meals at the
Priory. Max. stay 1 wk.

Guests Admitted To: Chapel to join the Sisters for daily
Eucharist and the Divine Office. Grounds.

Of Interest: St. Hilda's Priory is the Mother House of the
Order of the Holy Paraclete, founded in Whitby in 1915.
Dedicated to the Holy Spirit, the Sisters' daily life is centered on
prayer. The great Abbey on the East Cliff of Whitby reminds
them of their heritage and their patron, St. Hilda, whose
concerns for education, culture and Christian unity are as real
today as in the latter part of the 7th c. Hilda, a wise leader of
her day, ruled over a double monastery of both men and women.

Access: Road: 1.6 km. from Whitby Town Center. See O.H.P.
St. Oswald's Pastoral Center for road and rail access.

Order of the Holy Paraclete
St. Oswald's Pastoral Center
Woodland's Drive
Sleights, **Whitby**
North Yorks YO21 1RY
Anglican

Tel: 01947 810496
Fax: 01947 810750
Contact: Sister in Charge

Open To: Individuals, groups for Retreats, Day Events, and for a quiet place for rest and study.

Accommodation: Hospitality is provided in this small complex for up to 12 persons. Kitchen, lounges, library. In a separate building, The Grimston Room holds up to 40 persons for day programs.

Guests Admitted To: Chapel. Grounds.

Of Interest: St. Oswald's Pastoral Center is situated in the village of Sleights in the Esk Valley on the edge of the North Yorkshire Moors. The house is surrounded by beautiful countryside that is ideal for walking. Within easy reach is Whitby Abbey (see O.H.P. St. Hilda's Priory).

Access: Rail: From Darlington and Middlesbrough to Whitby Sta., then bus or taxi from Town Center 4.8 km. Road: A171, A169, B1460, B1416. By coach from York, bus from Scarborough. Local buses from Whitby.

Stanbrook Abbey
Callow End
Worcester WR2 4TD
Roman Catholic Benedictine

Tel: 01905 830307
Fax: 01905 831737
Contact: The Warden

Open To: Individuals, groups for Retreats. Day or residential use. Spiritual Direction available.

Accommodation: Hospitality is provided in St. Mary's House for 18 persons, 1 en-suite ground floor bedroom. Meals taken in Guest House. Oratory, library, quiet room. Also, if desired, The Presbytery offers separate facilities for clergy/male religious. Meals taken with other guests.

Guests Admitted To: Abbey Church.

Of Interest: The Community of Nuns now at Stanbrook Abbey was founded in 1623. First-time guests are invited to meet with the Guest Mistress or one of her assistants. The Silence lasts from 20:15 to 07:45. Voices are kept low and conversation ceases by 22:30. There are good country walks nearby, and the village of Callow End is of historic interest.

Access: Road: A449 from Worcester 6.4 km. Turn off onto B4424. House is on right at entrance to village. Good public transport.

St. Bede's Pastoral Center
21 Blossom Street
York YO24 1AQ

Tel: 01904 610446
Fax: 01904 655813
Contact: Administrator

Open To: Groups for Prayer Meetings, Courses on Spirituality; individuals or groups for Quiet Days. A member of the Community may be available for Spiritual Direction or prayer.

Accommodation: Non-residential. B&B available at the adjoining Bar Convent – Tel: 01904 629359.

Guests Admitted To: Center Chapel for weekday Mass.

Of Interest: St. Bede's is an ecumenical center administered by The Institute of the Blessed Virgin Mary, a Community of Roman Catholic Sisters. Lay administrators undertake the day to day running. The Sisters have been at the Bar Convent, York since 1686. Benedictine monks initiated St. Bede's Pastoral Center, and when they left in 1994, the Sisters came into residence.

Access: Rail: York Railway Sta. and York Bus Sta., both approx. 5 min. on foot from the Center. York is on the main rail line from London to Edinburgh.

Ireland

Ballintubber Abbey Retreat Experience
Ballintubber   Tel: 094 30934
Claremorris   Fax: 094 30018
Co. Mayo   Contact: Secretary
Roman Catholic
E-mail:btubabbey@tinet.ie

Open To: Individuals, groups for Retreats, May – Sept. The Retreat Experience consists of: Prayerful Solitude on Church Island; Exploration and Reflection on Tochar Phadraig; Reading and Meditation in Ballintubber Abbey and Grounds.

Accommodation: Locally in B&B's, hostel, self-catering houses.

Guests Admitted To: Ballintubber Abbey, Ireland's only Royal Abbey, in continuous use for over 782 years. Grounds landscaped to portray spiritual themes and as a resource for Retreats.

Of Interest: The old pilgrim path, Tochar Phadraig, runs from Ballintubber Abbey to Croagh Patrick, Ireland's Holy Mountain. The path is named after St. Patrick, Ireland's patron saint. However, it predates Christianity and was probably built around 350 AD. The route is some 35.2 km. long and passes through unspoiled countryside, dotted with ancient monuments, pre-famine villages and historic castles. A retreatant does not necessarily have to walk the Tochar. The monastic site on Church Island, situated in nearby Lough Carra, has been restored. St. Finian founded a church on the island in the 6th c. This small wooded island is accessible by boat and is also a place of retreat.

Access: Air: Knock Airport, then an 80 km. drive.
Rail: Nearest Sta. at Castlebar. Road: N34 to Castlebar, then 12.8 km. to Ballintubber.

Loreto House, Peace and Reconciliation Center
Linsfort, **Buncrana**   Tel: 077 62204
Co. Donegal   Fax: 077 62932
Roman Catholic   Contact: Sr. Anne McDaid, IBVM
E-mail:amcdaid@tinet.ie

Open To: Individuals, married couples, small groups for
Retreats, Meetings, and for those seeking rest and relaxation in
a peaceful, beautiful setting. Varying lengths of stay.

Accommodation: Hospitality is provided in 10 bedrooms, 5
en-suite. Dining room, solarium, living room. Non-residential
conference facilities for small groups. Aroma therapist/Reflex-
ologist on Mondays.

Guests Admitted To: Chapel. Grounds.

Of Interest: Loreto House is situated in the country beneath
the Hills of Donegal on the east shore of Lough Swilly. This
area is ideal for quiet walks through the countryside.

Access: Rail: Northern Inland Rail to Waterside and Derry.
Coach service to Derry, Buncrana and Letterkenny. Road:
National routes to Derry or Letterkenny, then follow signs for
Buncrana north to Linsfort. Local bus, mini-bus and taxi
service. Buncrana 8 km.

Mount Melleray Abbey
Cappoquin
Co. Waterford
Roman Catholic Cistercian

Tel: 058 54404
Contact: Guestmaster

Open To: Individuals, mostly the indigenous population for Private Retreats. Day visitors welcome.

Accommodation: Hospitality is provided in the Retreat House for approx. 30 persons. Meals taken in dining room. Guests free to structure their own time.

Guests Admitted To: Abbey Church to join the monks for Mass and the Divine Office. Grounds.

Of Interest: Mount Melleray Abbey was the first monastery founded in Ireland after the Reformation. Prior to that time, young men seeking to become monks went to the Cistercian Monastery of Melleray in Brittany, France. On November 30, 1831, all foreign monks at Melleray were forced to leave by the French Government. In December, sixty four Irish and English monks returned to Ireland with their Prior. They were given a tract of mountainous land near Cappoquin, Co. Waterford, and in 1832, Mount Melleray Abbey was founded. It is situated on the slopes of the Knockmealdown Mountains on six hundred acres, some used for dairy farming by the monks.

Access: Rail: From Dublin to Mallow, then by bus to the small town of Cappoquin. Abbey 8 km. Road: By bus from Dublin or Cork to Dungarvan, the largest town nearby, then 24 km. by taxi to the Abbey.

St. Benedict's Priory   Tel: 021 811354
The Mount   Contact: Prioress
Cobh, Co. Cork
Roman Catholic Benedictines
Adorers of the Sacred Heart of Jesus of Montmartre

Open To: Individuals for Private Retreats, Days of
Recollection. Small groups by prior arrangement.

Accommodation: Hospitality is provided in the Priory in 6
single bedrooms, 2 double. Dinner provided by the Community.
Other meals may be self-catered from stores on hand.

Guests Admitted To: Oratory. Monastic Heritage Exhibit.
Craft Shop. Bible Garden. Resurrection Garden. Garden of
Olives. Garden of Song. Vineyard.

Of Interest: The Priory's Monastic Heritage Exhibit describes
the story of monasticism in Ireland. The Bible Garden covers
one and one half acres and has trees, shrubs and flowers
mentioned in the Bible. A relic of St. Oliver Plunket is housed
in a reliquary in the oratory, a place of pilgrimage and prayer
for peace in Ireland. The Sisters sell homemade cakes, jams
and chutneys in the Craft Shop which is open daily.
Information about their Motherhouse, Tyburn Convent, can be
found at www.tyburnconvent.org.uk.

Access: Rail: To Cobh Sta. from Cork City, then a short walk
uphill. Road: N25 from Wexford, exit in direction of Cobh. N8
from Dublin, Cobh exit. N20 from Limerick.

Bessboro Retreat Center and Sacred Heart Convent
Bessboro, Blackrock
Cork
Roman Catholic
Srs. of the Sacred Heart

Tel: 021 375730
Contact: Director

Open To: Non-residential groups for Retreats, Conferences, Workshops. Also, individuals for Private Retreats.

Accommodation: Hospitality is provided for day programs in the Center. Conference rooms, meeting rooms. Restaurant serving up to 50 persons across the courtyard. Also, residential accommodations for one person in self-catering log cabin with kitchenette, bedroom, bath. Small groups (up to 10) may use cabin for the day.

Guests Admitted To: Chapel. Grounds.

Of Interest: The Center and Convent are situated close to Cork City Center, and Cork Heritage Park is nearby for walks among lovely gardens and woodland.

Access: Road: From Douglas, turn R onto Skehard Rd., then R on Bessboro Rd. to the Center. From Mahon to intersection of Skehard and Bessboro Rds., then L.

Poor Clare Monastery   Contact: Abbess
College Road
Cork
Roman Catholic Poor Clares
Franciscan/Colettines

Open To: Visitors wishing to join the Sisters for liturgical
services or speak with a member of the Community in the
parlour during visiting hours.

Accommodation: None at the monastery.

Guests Admitted To: Chapel for Holy Mass daily. Rosary
17:30 daily. Sunday Evening Prayer, Rosary and Benediction
16:40. Daily Exposition of the Blessed Sacrament 07:00 – 18:00.

Of Interest: This Poor Clare Monastery was founded on
Christmas night in 1914.

Access: Contact for further information.

O marvellous humility,
O astonishing poverty!
The king of angels—
the Lord of heaven
and earth is laid in a manger! (St.Clare)

St. Dominic's Retreat House
Ennismore, Montenotte
Cork City
Roman Catholic Dominican

Tel: 021 502520
Fax: 021 502712
Contact: The Secretary

Open To: Individuals, groups, students for Retreats or Holiday.

Accommodation: Hospitality is provided in the Priory in 40 single bedrooms, 2 double, lift. Conference rooms, group rooms, library. The self-catering Hermitage is a semi-Georgian cottage for those seeking the Lord in silence. The self-catering Meditation Center is for groups, with 2 Georgian stables converted into bunkhouses. Kitchen, large hall, prayer room, craft room, showers/toilets.

Guests Admitted To: Chapel. Grounds.

Of Interest: St. Dominic's is situated in thirty acres of beautiful woods, fields and gardens overlooking Lough Mahon. It is a twenty minute walk from the City Center. The cut stone buildings of the Meditation Center date from 1824 and were restored in 1987. The Center is two hundred yards from the main house.

Access: Air: Airport 20 min. away. Rail: Sta. 5 min. by taxi or Bus #8 – stops at Mayfield Green near Center. Road: City Center to Silver Springs Colmcille Lane exit, then L on Colmcille Ave. and follow signs for St. Dominic's.

Monastery of St. Catherine of Siena   Tel: 041 9838524
The Twenties   Contact: Prioress
Drogheda, Louth
Roman Catholic Dominican

Open To: Individuals, small groups for Retreats. Public welcome to attend liturgical services in the Chapel, open 07:00 – 19:00, and to pray before the Blessed Sacrament.

Accommodation: Hospitality is provided in the self-catering Retreat House in 4 single en-suite bedrooms. Retreatants bring their own food and toiletries. Oratory with Blessed Sacrament reserved.

Guests Admitted To: Monastery Chapel to join the Sisters for Mass and Divine Office. Exposition of the Blessed Sacrament.

Of Interest: In response to the desire of the Church that those dedicated to the contemplative life should share their life of prayer, the nuns offer this possibility through the Retreat House. The keeping of silence is very important in consideration of other retreatants; therefore, earphones must be used with recorder or radio.

Access: Air: Dublin Airport, then a 40 min. drive. Rail: Very good train and bus service between Dublin and Drogheda. Road: Take the main Dublin – Belfast Rd., then approx. 1.6 km. after you turn off for the Monastery.

AVILA, Carmelite Centre of Spirituality   Tel: 01 6683155
Morehampton Road   Fax: 01 6687618
6687618
Donnybrook
Dublin 4
Roman Catholic Discalced Carmelite Friars (O.C.D.)
E-mail:AvilaRetreat@tinet.ie

Avila is dedicated to serving the Church by promoting the spiritual life through prayer and instruction on the Christian life. To foster this aim, it provides a prayerful atmosphere of peace and quiet and organizes retreats, courses and seminars. These activities, unless otherwise stated, are open to all. The house is available at other times for groups who may wish to use the facilities for spiritual purposes. Avila has residential accommodation in single rooms for 47 people. All floors are accessible by a lift.

DEEP PEACE OF THE RUNNING WAVE TO YOU. DEEP PEACE OF THE FLOWING AIR TO YOU. DEEP PEACE OF THE QUIET EARTH TO YOU. DEEP PEACE OF THE SON OF PEACE TO YOU.

A Gaelic Blessing

Marianella, Center for Study and Renewal
75 Orwell Road   Tel: 01 4067100
Dublin 6   Fax: 01 4929635
Roman Catholic Redemptorists   Contact: Director

Open To: Men and women engaged in ministry for Courses, Retreats. Send for current calendar.

Accommodation: Hospitality is provided in the Center for course participants. Meals taken in dining room with the resident community.

Guests Admitted To: Chapel to join the Community for Mass and Divine Office. Grounds.

Of Interest: Marianella is home to a lively and welcoming Community with a varied apostolate. The programs are enriched by the diversity of persons who come for renewal, study and development of pastoral skills. The Center is situated in a quiet residential suburb in the foothills of the Dublin Mountains. There are many cultural activities in the area such as sightseeing in Dublin on foot, and day trips to the Boyne Valley and Glendalough. Recreational activities include a well-equipped sports center next door, golf courses nearby, and swim facilities in local schools.

Access: Road: Center of Dublin 20 min. by car or bus.

Mercy Center   Tel: 8487259
St. Brendan's Drive   Fax: 8485934
Coolock   Contact: The Secretary
Dublin 5
Roman Catholic Sisters of Mercy

Open To: Groups for non-residential Retreats and Courses.
May bring their own facilitator.

Accommodation: Hospitality is provided for 30 adults in the
Center, located in the convent basement.

Guests Admitted To: Prayer Room.

Of Interest: Catherine McAuley, foundress of the Sisters of
Mercy, was born in Stormanstown House September 29, 1778.
When she was a young woman, Mr. and Mrs. Callaghan invited
her to live with them in Coolock House, and in time willed the
entire estate to her. She built the Baggot Street House, the first
convent, and attached was the first House of Mercy. Coolock
House was bought back by the Sisters in 1956, and an extension
was completed in 1963. Visitors should make prior arrange-
ments with the Sisters to view the house.

Access: Road: Buses #27, 27A, 17A, 42, 42C to Coolock Village.

Teach Chaoimhin and Teach Lorcain   Tel: 01 8725055
Glendalough   Fax: 01 8725010
County Wicklow   Contact: Director
                                      Catholic Youth Council
                                      Arran Quay
                                      Dublin 7

Open To: Young adults wishing to meet as a Christian
Community in a House of Prayer.

Accommodation: Hospitality is provided in 3 dormitories for
30 persons at Teach Chaoimhin and in 8 single bedrooms at
Teach Lorcain. Self-catered meals by the group using the
facilities.

Guests Admitted To: House Chapel. Grounds.

Of Interest: In the 6th c., St. Kevin founded a monastery in
this beautiful, secluded and peaceful Glendasan Valley.
St. Laurence O'Toole also lived in that monastic community.
Both are patron saints of Dublin. The Catholic Youth Council is
the Dublin diocesan youth service. It calls young people to be
disciples of Jesus Christ and seeks creative ways to announce
the Gospel to them. CYC has been involved in ongoing pilgrimages abroad, especially to Taize and World Youth Days.

Access: Road: Car or bus to Glendalough.

Our Lady of Knock Shrine
Knock
County Mayo
Roman Catholic

Tel: 094 88100
Fax: 094 88295
Contact: Secretary
Shrine Office

Open To: Pilgrims year round. Pilgrimage Season with ceremonies at 15:00 April – October. National Public Novena August 14th – 22nd. Confessions available 5 to 8 hours daily.

Accommodation: Locally.

Pilgrims Welcome To: Grounds, Basilica, the three Chapels and all facilities.

Of Interest: On Thursday evening, August 21, 1879, Our Blessed Mother, St. Joseph, and St. John the Evangelist appeared on the external gable of the small church at Knock. To the right of the figures the witnesses saw the figure of a Lamb on an altar behind which there was a cross. The figures were surrounded by a brilliant light. The witnesses heard no voice nor did they receive any interior message or sign. The focus of the Apparition was obviously on the altar and the figure of a Lamb. To the west of Knock Shrine is St. Patrick's Holy Hill, 'the Reek', site of an annual Croagh Patrick Pilgrimage on the last Sunday of July.

Access: Rail or Bus: From Dublin or any of the other cities or towns. Road: Dublin 3 hrs. by car. Cork or Belfast 4 hrs.

St. Catherine Laboure Holiday Home   Tel: 094 88262
Knock   Contact: Administrator
County Mayo
Roman Catholic Society of St. Vincent De Paul

Open To: Senior citizens March – Nov. – one week stay. For others, check with administrator about availability of short-stay accommodations.

Accommodation: Hospitality is provided in the Guest House for 25 persons in single and twin-bedded rooms. B&B and/or full-board.

Of Interest: Knock Village is situated on a hilltop overlooking lake-studded bogland, with views of the Ox Mountains, of Sligo to the north, and the Twelve Bens of Connemara to the south-west. There are walking paths from the Holiday Home leading to Our Lady's Shrine.

Access: Rail: Claremorris Sta., then by bus or taxi. Road: 1 h. from Galway and from Sligo by car, 3 h. from Dublin, 4 h. from Cork.

Drumalis Retreat and Conference Center
Glenarm Road, **Larne**   Tel: 01574 272196/276455
Co. Antrim BT40 1DT   Fax: 01574 277999
Northern Ireland   E-mail:drumalis@dial.pipex.com
Roman Catholic   Contact: Retreat Secretary
Inter-Faith – Cross Community
Sisters of the Cross and Passion
Website:http://dspace.dial.pipex.com/drumalis

Open To: Individuals, groups for Retreats, Days of Prayer.
Spiritual Direction available.

Accommodation: Hospitality is provided in the Center for up
to 100 persons. Conference rooms, prayer rooms, small group
rooms. *Parkview,* a small Gate Lodge, sleeps 5 and is self-
catering.

Guests Admitted To: Chapels. Library. Spacious grounds.

Of Interest: The Congregation of the Sisters of the Cross and
Passion was founded in 1851 in Manchester, England.
Drumalis occupies the site of a 12th c. Premonstratensian Priory
which was suppressed in 1591. The present house was built in
1892. It is situated on the beautiful Antrim Coast overlooking
the sea.

Access: Rail or Bus: Regular bus and train services from
Belfast. Road: M2 from Belfast, then exit A8. Turn L onto
Pound St. – Victoria Rd. Drumalis is at the end of the road.

Bolton Abbey   Tel: 0507 24104
Moone (Athy)   Fax: 0505 24309
County Kildare   Contact: Guestmaster
Roman Catholic Cistercian

Open To: Individuals wishing to share to some extent in the life of the monks.

Accommodation: Hospitality is provided in the Guest House in 8 single bedrooms. Meals taken in guest dining room. Max. length of stay one week.

Guests Admitted To: Abbey Church for Mass and Divine Office. Garden areas and paths through the farm for quiet walks.

Of Interest: Bolton Abbey was founded in 1965 from Mount St. Joseph Abbey, Roscrea, Co. Tipperary. It is situated on the site of a 15th c. castle comprising two tower houses, one still inhabited by the monks. Nearby in what were Celtic monasteries are the High Crosses of Castledermot and the world famous Moone High Cross. Eight kilometers east are the ruins of Baltinglass Abbey, the second Cistercian foundation in Ireland. The Community's main source of livelihood is the two hundred and fifty acre dairy farm. The Abbey is located in the outer foothills of the Wicklow Mountains.

Access: Road: Naas-Carlow Rd., then 1.6 km. past the village of Moone. Follow signpost for Bolton Abbey. The Abbey is 1.6 km. off the main road.

Glenstal Abbey
Murroe
County Limerick
Roman Catholic Cistercian

Tel: 061 386103
Fax: 061 386328
Contact: Guestmaster

Open To: Individuals for Private Retreats.

Accommodation: Hospitality is provided in the small Guest House.

Guests Admitted To: Abbey Church to join the monks for Mass and Divine Office. Icon Chapel (by arrangement). Bible Garden (by arrangement). Gift Shop.

Of Interest: In medieval times, this site belonged to the Cistercian Abbey of Owney. Glenstal Abbey was founded in 1927 from the Abbey of Maredsous in Belgium. The monks have maintained a tradition of arts and crafts, with special emphasis on metalwork, sculpture and woodturning.

Access: Contact for further information.

St. Patrick's Purgatory   Tel/Fax: 353 72 61518
Lough Derg   Contact: Prior
Pettigo
County Donegal
Roman Catholic

Open To: Pilgrims, 15 yrs. and older, June 1 – Aug. 15, for the Three-Day Pilgrimage. Days of Prayer for adults May and Sept. Private Retreats Oct. – Mar. Reservations required.

Accommodation: Hospitality is provided in houses and hostels on the island. Boats run at different schedules a.m. and p.m.

Guests Admitted To: Church on the island.

Of Interest: St. Patrick's Purgatory, situated on an island of a remote lake, has a long history dating back to medieval times. It is one of the most demanding pilgrimages in the Christian world. Pilgrims walk barefoot, fast from midnight prior to arrival, and are allowed only one meal a day.

Access: Road: From Enniskillen, 32 km. Belleek 32 km. Omagh 44.8 km. Pettigo 6.4 km. from St. Patrick's Purgatory.

Our Lady of Bethlehem Abbey
11 Ballymena Road
Portglenone, Ballymena
County Antrim BT44 8BL
Northern Ireland
Roman Catholic Cistercian

Tel: 44 028 2582 1211
Fax: 44 028 2582 2795
Contact: Guestmaster
E-mail: - kelly@unite.net

Open To: Individuals for Private Retreats. Spiritual Direction available. Day visitors welcome.

Accommodation: Hospitality is provided in the Guest House in 8 bedrooms (12 beds). Meals taken in Guest House dining room.

Guests Admitted To: Public Church only in normal circumstances.

Of Interest: Our Lady of Bethlehem Abbey was founded in 1948 from Mount Melleray Abbey. It is situated on the banks of the Lower Bann River. The monks support themselves through their Guest House apostolate, repository and craft shops, and printing.

Access: Road: M2 from Belfast. Follow signs for Randalstown/Portglenone.

LaVerna House, Center of Peace and Reconciliation
Rossnowlagh Tel: 072 51342/52035
County Donegal Fax: 072 52206
Roman Catholic Franciscan Contact: The Secretary

Open To: Individuals, groups for Retreats or for a short stay.

Accommodation: Hospitality is provided in LaVerna House. Library.

Guests Admitted To: Church to join the Friars for liturgical services. Grounds.

Of Interest: In the Spirit of St. Francis, the Franciscan Friars welcome those who long for that peace the world cannot give, and wish to share with them the beauty and serenity of this blessed place by the sea. Their Mission Statement is: 'Our calling is to heal wounds – to reunite those divided by enmity or misunderstanding – to lead back home those who have lost their way.'

Access: Road: 8 km. from Ballyshannon on Rossnowlagh Rd. From Donegal Town, take Ballyshannon Rd., turn R (signpost at Ballintra). No public transport to Rossnowlagh. Pickup may be possible at Ballyshannon with advance notice.

PRAISE AND BLESS MY LORD · THANK HIM TOO AND SERVE HIM IN GREAT HUMILITY. St. Francis.

St. Mary's Abbey
Glencairn, **Tallow**
County Waterford
Roman Catholic Cistercian

Tel: 058 56168
Fax: 058 56616
Contact: Guest Mistress

Open To: Family, friends, priests and religious for Private Retreats or a quiet time apart. Day visitors welcome to join the Sisters for liturgical services.

Accommodation: Hospitality is provided in the small Guest House in 3 bedrooms. Book well in advance. Accommodation available for visitors to the Abbey in Lismore, the closest town.

Guests Admitted To: Abbey Church for Mass and Divine Office.

Of Interest: Glencairn was originally built in 1619. It was purchased in 1926 by Mount Melleray Abbey for Cistercian nuns, the first in Ireland since the Reformation. St. Mary's Abbey was founded in 1932 from Holy Cross Abbey, Stapehill, Dorset, England. The Sisters have close ties with Mount Melleray, located 6.4 km. away. Their sources of income are the Eucharistic Bread Department and the dairy herd. It is situated on the banks of the River Blackwater.

Access: Road: From Cappoquin, Waterford, Dublin, etc., turn R at monument in Lismore, 4.8 km. from the Abbey, and take R fork at Hornibrooks.

Mount Tabor Hermitage   Tel/Fax: 098 21599
Drummin, **Westport**   Contact: Guest Sister
County Mayo
Traditional Roman Catholic (Tridentine Rite)
Taborite Nuns of Mary Immaculate

Open To: Individuals for Retreats. Guests are free to schedule
their own time. May assist with manual labor as desired.
Length of stay variable.

Accommodation: Hospitality is provided in self-catering
hermitages. Bring food – (bed linens if possible).

Guests Admitted To: Sisters' Chapel for daily Eucharist,
Adoration, and Divine Office. Holy Sacrifice of the Mass each
Saturday (Traditional Latin Rite). Library. Drummin Church
for Sunday Mass. Grounds.

Of Interest: The Hermitage is situated in a rich, forestry
plantation under the shadow of Croagh Patrick and the Sheefry
Hills in the Drummin Valley near the Owenmore River. An old
abandoned farmhouse was purchased from Irish Forestation in
1992 and restored – a unique environment for a Desert Retreat.

Access: Road: N60 to Westport, exit onto N59. Turn off at
Liscarney in direction of Delphi. Take a R at Drummin Church
and follow signs to the Hermitage.

HERITAGE SITES

Duchas The Heritage Service is the State body responsible for the protection and conservation of Ireland's natural and built heritage. It is part of the Department of Arts, Heritage, Gaeltacht and the islands. For further information, contact:
Education & Visitor Service
51 St. Stephen's Green
Dublin 2, Ireland
Tel: 353 1 661 3111   Fax: 353 1 661 6764
E-mail:visits@indigo.ie

Ennis Friary   Tel: 065 29100
Abbey Street, Ennis Town
County Clare

Open: Late May – Sept. Guided Tour available on request. Public coach/car park closeby. Contact for current charges.

Of Interest: Ennis Friary was founded in the 13th c. by the O'Brien's. There are many 15th – 16th c. sculptures carved in the local limestone, such as the figure of St. Francis depicting the stigmata.

Scattery Island Centre   Tel: 065 52144/52139
Merchants Quay, Kilrush
County Clare

Open: Mid-June – Sept. Free of charge.

Of Interest: This information center on the mainland interprets the island on which a monastery is situated. It was founded by St. Senan in the 6th c. and consists of a round tower and several churches.

Lusk Heritage Centre   Tel: 01 843 7683
Lusk
County Dublin

Open: Fridays only, mid-June – Sept. Guided Tour available
on request. Contact for current charges.

Of Interest: Lusk Heritage Centre consists of a 9th c. round
tower, a medieval belfry, and a 19th c. church. The belfry houses
an exhibit of medieval churches of North Co. Dublin.

Access: Road: Bus Rt. 33 from City Center, 1 h.

St. Mary's Abbey   Tel: 01 872 1490
Chapter House, Meetinghouse Lane
Off Capel Street
Dublin 1

Open: Mid-June – Sept. Guided Tour available on request.
Contact for current charges.

Of Interest: St. Mary's Abbey was founded in 1139 by the
Benedictine Monastery of Savigny, France. It became a
Cistercian foundation in 1147, and was one of the most
important monasteries in Ireland until its suppression in the
16th c. The exhibit has been put together by Duchas the
Heritage Service as well as the Dublin Archaeological Society
and the History of Art Department at Trinity College, Dublin.

Access: Road: From O'Connell St., down Abbey St., cross
Capel St. to a street named Mary's Abbey. Turn R into Meetinghouse Lane. Located in the center of Dublin.

Ardfert Cathedral   Tel: 066 34711
Ardfert
County Kerry

Open: Early May – Sept. Guided Tour available on request.
Contact for current charges.

Of Interest: St. Brendan 'the Navigator' founded a monastery
here in the 6th c. There are three medieval churches, an ogham
stone, and many early Christian and medieval grave slabs on
site. The cathedral dates from the 12th – 17th c. The battle-
ments were added in the 15th c.

Access: Road: R551 (Tralee to Ballyheigue Rd.), 10 km.

Gallarus Oratory
Dingle Peninsula
County Kerry

Open: Mid-June – Sept. Free of charge.

Of Interest: Gallarus Oratory is the most perfectly preserved
boat-shaped oratory in Co. Kerry, built between the 9th – 12th c.
It resembles an upturned boat, with drystone walls.

Access: Road: Off R559.

Muckross Friary   Tel: 064 31440
Muckross Estate
Killarney
County Kerry

Open: Mid-June – Sept. Free of charge. Public car park closeby.

Of Interest: This Franciscan Friary was founded in the 15th c. The tower, added after the church was built, is the only Franciscan tower in Ireland as wide as the church. The cloister and buildings are complete. The friars were dispelled in 1652.

Access: Road: N71 (Kenmare Rd.), then a 5-10 min. walk from car park near Muckross Hotel. Killarney 4 km.

Jerpoint Abbey   Tel: 056 24623
Thomastown
County Kilkenny

Open: Mid-Mar. – Oct. Guided Tour available on request. Contact for current charges.

Of Interest: This Cistercian Abbey was founded in the 12th c. The church dates from this period, the tower and cloister from the 15th c. There are unique carvings iin the sculptured cloister arcade.

Access: Road: N9, 2.5 km. SW of Thomastown.

Old Mellifont Abbey   Tel: 041 26459
Tullyallen
County Louth

Open: May – Oct. Guided Tour available on request. Self-guiding trail. Public car/coach park. Picnic area. Contact for current charges.

Of Interest: This was the first Cistercian Monastery in Ireland, founded in 1142 by St. Malachy of Armagh. It has an interesting octagonal lavabo. The Visitor Centre houses an exhibit on the work of masons in the Middle Ages.

Access: Road: Off the main Drogheda-Collon Rd.

Clonmacnoise   Tel: 0905 74195
Shannonbridge   Fax: 0905 74273
County Offaly

Open: Year round, except Christmas Day. Guided Tour available on request. Visitor Centre – exhibits – audio-visual presentation. Car/coach park. Restaurant/tearoom. Contact for current charges.

Of Interest: Clonmacnoise is an early Christian site founded by St. Claran in the 6th c. on the banks of the Shannon River. The site includes the ruins of a cathedral, eight churches (10th – 13th c.), two round towers, three high crosses, and a large collection of early Christian grave slabs.

Access: Road: N62, 21 km. from Athlone. R357, 20 km. from Ballinasloe.

Boyle Abbey   Tel: 079 62604
Boyle Town
County Roscommon

Open: June – Sept. Guided Tours. Exhibit in restored Gate
House (16th – 17th c.). Car/coach park closeby. Contact for
current charges.

Of Interest: This well-preserved Cistercian Monastery was
founded in the 12th c. under the patronage of the MacDermott
family. It was damaged during the 17th – 18th c. when it housed
a military garrison.

Access: Road: Off N4 (Dublin – Sligo Rd.).

Sligo Abbey   Tel: 071 46406
Abbey Street, Sligo
County Sligo

Open: Mid-June – Sept. Guided Tour available on request.
Exhibits. Public car/coach park closeby. Contact for current
charges.

Of Interest: This Dominican Friary was founded in the 13th c.
by Maurice FitzGerald. It contains a wealth of carvings, well-
preserved cloisters, and the only surviving sculptured 15th c.
high altar in any Irish monastic church.

Access: Located in the center of Sligo Town.

Rock of Cashel   Tel: 062 61437
Cashel
County Tipperary

Open: Year round. Guided Tour available on request.
Exhibits. Audio-visual presentation – 'Stronghold of the Faith'.
Car/coach park closeby. Contact for current charges.

Of Interest: This group of buildings is situated on limestone in
the Golden Vale. It includes a 12th c. round tower, High Cross
and Romanesque Chapel, 13th c. Gothic Cathedral, 15th c. castle,
and the restored Hall of the Vicars Choral.

Access: Road: Off Dublin Rd., 500 m. from center of Cashel
Town.

Tintern Abbey   Tel: 01 661 3111
Saltmills, New Ross
County Wexford

Open: Contact for times and current charges. Guided Tour
available on request. Exhibits. Car park.

Of Interest: This Cistercian Abbey was founded in 1200 by
William, the Earl Marshall, and named after Tintern in Wales.
The site consists of nave, chancel, tower, chapel and cloister. It
was partly converted to living quarters from the 16th c. to the
1960's.

Access: Road: Off R734, 16 km. S of New Ross. Off R733
(Wexford to Ballyhack Rd.), 29 km. from Wexford.

Glendalough Visitor Centre   Tel: 0404 45325/45352
Glendalough, Bray   Fax: 0404 45626
County Wicklow

Open: Year round. Guided Tour available on request. Self-guiding trail. Exhibit. Audio-visual presentation – 'Ireland of the Monasteries'. Car/coach/bicycle park. Picnic area. Contact for current charges.

Of Interest: This early Christian monastic site was founded by St. Kevin in the 6th c. It is situated in a glaciated valley with two lakes. The site contains a round tower, stone churches, and decorated crosses in the graveyard.

Access: Road: R755, S of Dublin.

Scotland

Bishop's House, Isle of Iona   Tel: 01681 700800
Argyll PA76 6SJ   Fax: 01681 700801
Scottish Episcopal Church   Contact: The Warden
    E-mail:bhiona@aol.com

Open To: Individuals, groups, families for Retreats, and for those who wish to have a quiet holiday in a Christian environment. Main Season Mar. – Oct. Bookings at other times are considered if practical. Send for current tariff.

Accommodation: Hospitality is provided for 23 persons in 3 single bedrooms, 3 double, 7 twin, many with wash basins. Dining room, lounge. Guests are asked to contribute to light communal tasks. Min. stay 3 nights.

Guests Admitted To: Chapel of St. Columba (central part of house) for worship services. Grounds.

Of Interest: Bishop's House is one of two houses operated under the auspices of the Diocese of Argyll and The Isles. The other house is located on the Island of Cumbrae, in the Firth of Clyde, at The College, Millport. When Alexander Chinnery-Haldane, Bishop of Argyll and The Isles, founded Bishop's House in 1894, he saw Iona as a house of prayer, study, contemplation, and Eucharist from which the light of the Gospel would spread around the world. This place of natural beauty and peace has been steeped in Christian prayer for fourteen centuries. Aside from the small village community, most of Iona remains as it was when St. Columba founded a Celtic monastery in 563 AD, spreading the Christian faith throughout Scotland and beyond. The ruins of a nunnery and other ancient Christian and pre-Christian sites are also found on the island, now owned by the National Trust.

Access: (See page 84) No cars allowed on Iona. Parking at Fionnphort.

The Iona Community   Tel: 01681 700404
Iona Abbey   Fax: 01681 700460
Isle of Iona   Contact: Bookings Secretary
Argyll PA76 6SN   E-mail:ionacomm@iona.org.uk
Ecumenical

Open To: Individuals, families, groups wishing to participate in the varied selection of Program Weeks or Open Weeks. Send for current information. Pilgrimage around Iona Wednesdays. Organized activities for children ages 3 – 14 while adults in session during *Experiencing Easter* and June – Sept. Staffed by The Resident Group and over 100 volunteers who participate in the life and worship of the Community for 6 – 16 wks. Inquiries about work as a resident or volunteer addressed to Abbey Staff Co-ordinator. Booking in writing up to a year in advance.

Accommodation: Hospitality is provided in the ancient Abbey for up to 45 persons in shared rooms mostly for 2, and in MacLeod Center in multi-bedded rooms (50 guests). Meals in refectory – guests help with communal tasks. Center facilities include a multi-purpose room, craft room, library, quiet room, and dark room (photographers). Also, camping available through Camas Adventure Camp in old cottages at an old fishing station on the Island of Mull. Contact: Camas Center, Bunessan, Mull PA67 6DX. Tel: 01681 700367. Open to group bookings mid-May – early Sept. Work Weeks and Open Weeks.

Of Interest: On Pentecost in 563 AD, Ireland's St. Columba landed on this small Hebridean island and made his mission base for the Celtic Church. This holy ground is considered the Cradle of Christianity for much of Scotland, Northern England and Europe. The Iona Community, founded in 1938 by The Very Reverend George MacLeod of Fuinary, is an Ecumenical Christian Community committed to seeking new ways of living the Gospel in today's world. Gathered around the rebuilding of the Benedictine Monastery, they live a common life of prayer and work that is Christ centered.

Access: Road: To Oban to catch noon ferry to Craignure on Mull Is., then car or bus to Fionnphort for Iona ferry.

Sancta Maria Abbey
Nunraw, Garvald
Haddington EH41 4LW
Roman Catholic Cistercian

Tel: 01620 830228
Contact: Guestmaster

Open To: Individuals, small groups for Retreats, or simply a time of rest and renewal in a monastic setting. Spiritual Direction available.

Accommodation: Hospitality is provided in the Guest House for up to 30 persons in single, double, and dormitory rooms. Max. stay 5 days.

Guests Admitted To: Chapel to join the monks for Mass and Divine Office. Grounds that are open to guests.

Of Interest: Sancta Maria Abbey was founded in 1946 from Mount St. Joseph Abbey, Roscrea, Ireland. There are opportunities for peaceful walks in the lovely countryside.

Access: Air: Edinburgh Airport 64 km.
Rail: Edinburgh Sta. 48 km.

Kilravock Castle Christian Center   Tel/Fax: 01667 493258
Croy   Contact: Castle Manager
Inverness IV2 7PJ
E-mail:Castles@Kilravock-Rose-freeserve.co.uk

Open To: Visitors and groups seeking accommodations and
fellowship in a comfortable and friendly Christian environment.
Meals served year round, but Guest House open April – Oct.
Meals offered to non-residents and groups by arrangement.

Accommodation: Hospitality is provided in the Castle and
East Wing, some en-suite, B&B and evening meals. Lunches
and snacks available on request. Library, laundry, sports
facilities on site. Also, a Granary Building – Youth Hostel –
houses approx. 40 people, including leader's room. Central heat,
well-equipped – year round.

Guests Admitted To: Baronial meals Sunday evenings,
banquet style, for guests and visitors by arrangement. Grounds.

Of Interest: Kilravock Castle is situated in extensive grounds
with a garden rich with ancient trees. The wild life and birds
have been described as spectacular.

Access: Air: Inverness Airport (Dalcross) 6.4 km. Road: Croy
3.2 km. Nairn 9.6 km. Inverness 19.2 km.

Benedictine Monastery
5 Mackerston Place
Largs
Ayrshire KA30 8BY
Roman Catholic
Adorers of the Sacred Heart of Jesus of Montmartre, OSB

Tel: 01475 687320
Contact: Prioress

Open To: Individuals for Retreats, or simply for a peaceful and quiet time apart. Guests are free to structure their own time.

Accommodation: Hospitality is provided in 10 single bedrooms, 1 double. Meals available.

Guests Admitted To: Chapel to join the Nuns for Mass and Divine Office. Exposition of the Blessed Sacrament.

Of Interest: The Priory's Christian Heritage Museum has much to offer that is related to Scotland's spiritual roots. Guests will enjoy the beautiful views overlooking Millport, and there are opportunities for refreshing walks along Largs' seafront.

Access: Ferry: Millport to Largs, then a 5-min. walk uphill. Rail: Glasgow to Largs Sta. (1 h.), then a 2-min. walk to the Priory. Road: From Glasgow along the Clyde Coast (40 min.).

St. Scholastica's Retreat   Tel: 0343 89375 (Retreat House)
Pluscarden Abbey   Fax: 0343 89257 (Abbey)
Elgin   Contact: The Warden (Retreat)
Moray IV30 3UA   Guestmaster (Abbey)
Roman Catholic Benedictine

Open To: Individuals, groups for Retreats. Groups may bring their own leader, or a more formal program may be organized by the Retreat House with prior arrangement. Spiritual Direction available. Booking by mail only.

Accommodation: Hospitality is provided for men in St. Benedict's, the Guest House Wing. Meals taken with the monks in the refectory. Women and groups are accommodated in St. Scholastica's in 12 bedrooms – 2 equipped for the handicapped. Sleeping bags appreciated. Shower rooms, self-catering guest kitchen. Basic foods stocked *(fresh produce in season)*.

Guests Admitted To: Abbey Church to join the Community for liturgical services. Grounds that are open to guests.

Of Interest: Pluscarden Abbey was founded in 1230 and refounded in 1948 from Prinknash Abbey, Gloucestershire. It is situated in lovely countryside, surrounded by forest land, hills, moors and fertile fields.

Access: Rail: Elgin Sta. 9.6 km. Road: A96. Buses Tues. and Fri. only.

Wales

Coleg Trefeca
Trefeca
Aberhonddu/**Brecon**
Powys LD3 0PP
Methodist/Presbyterian/Ecumenical

Tel/Fax: 01874 711423
Contact: The Warden

Open To: Individuals, groups for Retreats or simply a time away in a peaceful setting. Groups are advised to book at least 18 mos. in advance – 1 wk. in advance for individuals.

Accommodation: Hospitality is provided in the Conference Center for up to 38 persons. Full board can be provided for individuals when a group is in session *(meals taken with group)*.

Guests Admitted To: Center facilities, grounds. Museum.

Of Interest: This was home to Howell Harris, a leader of the 18th c. Methodist Revival in Wales. The small museum tells his story. The Center is situated on five rural acres, part of Brecon Beacons National Park in Mid-Wales.

Access: Road: Nearest city is Cardiff.

St. Deiniol's Library   Tel: 01244 532350
Hawarden, **Chester**   Fax: 01244 520643
Flintshire CH5 3DF   Contact: Administrator
E-mail:deiniol.visitors@btinternet.com

Open To: Scholars, clergy, educators from around the world.
Visiting scholars may use the facilities of University College
Chester. Individuals, groups wishing to attend courses,
seminars, day conferences arranged each year on a variety of
Theological and Victorian Studies themes with leading scholars.
Conference facilities available for residential or day groups. An
ideal environment for a Sabbatical. Also for those seeking a
relaxed place to study combined with holiday time.

Accommodation: Hospitality is provided in comfortable
bedrooms and pleasant surroundings. Meal service.

Guests Admitted To: Library *(collection contains most of
Gladstone's correspondence and speeches).* Library specializes in
Theology and History, with good collections of Literature,
Philosophy and Classics. The Bishop Moorman Franciscan
Collection is Britain's largest on St. Francis and the early
Franciscans. Chapel for morning prayer, evening prayer and
Eucharist.

Of Interest: William Ewart Gladstone (1809-1898) was
perhaps Britain's greatest statesman and the most significant
Anglican layman of the last two centuries. He lived in the
village of Hawarden in North Wales, the site of St. Deiniol's
Library which he founded in 1889 'for the pursuit of divine
learning'. The present Library was built as the national
memorial to Gladstone, unique in being a residential library –
bed, board and books. Gladstone wanted to gather a fellowship of scholars from all disciplines for solid and serious work
for the benefit of mankind in inexpensive lodgings together with
congenial society. He believed that where there is truth, there
is God, and that God's revelation could be found not only in
scripture but in the writings of the classical world, in the move-
ments of history, and in the insights of poets and novelists.

This search for truth is what Gladstone meant by divine learning. The Library is located near some of Britain's most beautiful contryside and ancient monuments – Snowdonia, the Roman City of Chester, and the castles and gardens of Wales.

Access: Road: Close to the English border. Contact for further information.

Carmelite Monastery   Tel: 0341 422546
Cader Road
Dolgellau
Gwynedd LL40 1SH
Roman Catholic

Open To: The public to stop and pray in the Chapel.

Accommodation: None at the monastery.

Guests Admitted To: Chapel. Extern Garden. Tea Room.

Of Interest: The Carmelite Monastery is located in a peaceful area with beautiful scenery. There are good walking trails and opportunities for fishing and golf in the area. Ruins of an abbey and an old gold mine are nearby. Harlech Castle and Blaenau Ffestiniog Slate Mines are within easy access. The Monastery is on the edge of the Snowdonia National Park.

Access: Rail: Machynlleth Sta. 28.8 km. Bus Sta. in Dolgellau 1.6 km.

The Holy Well of St. Winefride   Tel: 01352 713054
New Road
Holywell, Flintshire

Open To: Pilgrims, general public, for those wishing to visit
this place of unbroken pilgrimage for 1300 years. Open daily.

Accommodation: Hospitality is provided at St. Winefride's
Pilgrim's Rest, a few yards from the Holy Well. Contact Sister
Margaret at Tel: 01352 710763.

Pilgrims Admitted To: Chapel Crypt. Water at the Well.
Pilgrims pass through the water three times, an ancient custom
associated with the prayer of St. Winefride written in the 12th c.
for those who prayed at the Well – that their request may be
answered at least on the third time. There is also association
with the Celtic rite of baptizing by triple immersion.

Of Interest: St.Winefride was beheaded on this site, and St.
Beuno's Stone by the steps in the outer bath is where Beuno
prayed over her, placing her severed head beside her body. She
arose, a white scar encircling her neck as witness to her
martyrdom. Today's pilgrim kneels here to complete his prayers
after going through the water. Winefride became a nun, and in
time Abbess of a convent at Gwytherin near Llanrwst. She died
fifteen years later and was buried in a local churchyard. In
1138, her relics were removed to Shrewsbury Abbey.

Access: Road: A548 or A55, then follow signs for Holywell.

Poor Clare Colettine Monastery   Contact: Abbess
Hillside
Neath SA11 1TP
Roman Catholic Franciscan

Open To: Public for liturgical services. Opportunity to speak
with a member of the Community in the extern parlor.

Accommodation: None at the monastery.

Guests Admitted To: Chapel to join the Sisters for Mass.
Adoration of the Blessed Sacrament.

Of Interest: This Poor Clare Colettine Monastery was founded
in 1950 from the Monastery of St. Damian in Dublin. The small
chapel provides an opportunity for intimate prayer in an atmosphere of simplicity and silent antiquity expressive of the
medieval roots of the Poor Clares. The ruins of Neath Abbey are
nearby.

Access: Rail: Neath General Railway Sta., 10 min. on foot.
Taxis available. Road: Leave M4 at Jct. 41 (Briton Ferry
Bridge). Take A474 Briton Ferry to Neath. Turn R at Payne St.
then onto Darygraig Rd. to Hillside. Monastery on R just
before Highbury Court.

"CONTEMPLATE
the INEFFABLE   charity
that LED him   to suffer
ON the wood   of the cross
AND to die   there"
St. Clare

Catholic Centre for Healing in Marriage
Oasis of Peace   Tel: 01766 514300
Penamser Road, **Porthmadog**   Contact: Director
Gwynedd LL49 9NY

Open To: Maximum of six married couples for a unique growth experience. Courses Sun. – Fri: Second Honeymoon, Healing in Marriage, Growing Together, and Christian Holidays for Couples. Christian Counseling and Spiritual Direction.

Accommodation: Hospitality is provided in this comfortable home. Most rooms en-suite.

Guests Admitted To: Oratory for private prayer before the Blessed Sacrament. Gardens.

Of Interest: The Catholic Centre for Healing in Marriage is run by a lay community of couples called to a ministry of marriage, assisted by an ecclesiastical adviser. It is situated in beautiful countryside with mountains, lakes and sandy beaches on the edge of town in the Snowdonia National Park area of North Wales.

Access: Contact for further information.

Foster Place Retreat Centre   Tel: 01484 688680
Middle Foster Place   Contact: Retreat Secretary
Hepworth, Holmfirth
Huddersfield HD7 1TN
West Yorkshire, England

Open To: Individuals for Retreats, or simply a day away for rest and relaxation. Spiritual Direction, Counseling, and Psychotherapy available.

Accommodation: Hospitality is provided in the Centre. Meals taken with the staff.

Guests Admitted To: The Barn, Wed. evening to join the staff for a time of silence. Third Sun. of month for celebration of the Eucharist after a time of silence. Grounds.

Of Interest: Foster Place Retreat Centre, firmly rooted in the Christian tradition, is the focus of The Network for the Study of Spirituality. It provides a meeting place to explore ideas and approaches that assist the journey of the heart to God. The third Sunday during summer months, visitors may work with the staff in the garden and on the house. It is situated in the Holme Valley of the South Pennine Mountain Range.

Access: Road: A616 from Huddersfield to Sheffield. Located close to Hepworth.

Blessed St. Clare,
you trusted in the Blessed Sacrament
as your only protection.

In your hour of need
you heard a voice from the Sacred Host:

"I Will Always Take Care Of You"

Take care of us in our earthly needs.
Enkindle in us a tender love
for Jesus and Mary.

Plead for our families,
our beloved country,
and our suffering world.

Guide us by your light to heaven. Amen.

A PLACE APART

England
Ireland
Scotland
Wales

Late Entry Supplement

Ushaw College
Durham DH7 9RH
England
Roman Catholic
Partnerships with Anglican and Methodist Colleges

Tel/Fax: 0191 373 3499
www.dur.ac.uk/Ushaw
Contact: Rev. James O'Keefe
E-mail:J.P.O'Keefe@dur.ac.uk

Open To: Individuals, groups (residential and non-residential), families for Retreats, Conferences, Courses, and as a holiday base. Contact Course Administrator for further information about programs in Theology and Ministry, Spirituality, Liturgy and Scripture. Open year round.

Accommodation: Hospitality is provided in the Conference Center in 80 bedrooms, some en-suite. Four conference rooms, fully-equipped. Certain times of the year larger groups accommodated within main college buildings. Lecture theatre, swimming pool, conference rooms. Full catering for conferences, bar facilities, TV lounge

Guests Admitted To: Chapel. Grounds. From July 9 – 15, 2000, Journeying with Northern Saints I, and August 6 – 12, 2000, Journeying with Northern Saints II. Send for details about these Christian Heritage pilgrimages.

Of Interest: For almost two hundred years Ushaw College has specialized in education and formation for ministry , with its roots dating back to Douai, France and a College for training priests and laymen. Today Ushaw College responds to the formation needs of all the baptized in various ministries and callings. It is situated three miles west of Durham City, with its cathedral and castle, now a World Heritage Site, and other historic buildings, with easy access to ancient sites of the Northern Saints.

Access: Air: Newcastle Airport 40 km. Metrolink rail service from center of Newcastle to Durham. Rail: Durham Sta. 4.8 km., then by taxi. Road: From the south, A1(M) to north of Darlington, then A167 through traffic light at Neville's Cross to next traffic light. Turn left and follow sign for the college (4 km.). From the north, exit A1(M) at Chester-le-Street heading south on A167 to Crossgate Moor. Turn right at first traffic light past pedestrian footbridge, and continue on the road through village of Bearpark into the country. College on the right.